ANDREA GHISOTTI

THE RED

335 illustrations

All the marine species
illustrated in this book
were photographed by the author
in their natural habitat

BONECHI

CONTENTS

KEY

*The following graphic scheme is used for
the scientific nomenclature in the text:*

PHYLUM
Class
Subclass
ORDER
Family

Text by: Andrea Ghisotti
English translation: Kate Parenti
Scientific supervision and editing: Dott. Sabina Airoldi
Map: Studio Grafico Bellandi & Mariani, Pistoia

Photos by Andrea Ghisotti.
Page 124: a courtesy of Coral World Eilat
Page 125: archives of Casa Editrice Bonechi

ISBN 978-88-476-1418-5

Introduction

For Europeans, the Red Sea is their local tropical sea and it is served by numerous airline companies which allow them to reach the shores in only a few hours flight from all the most important European cities. The political stability of the northern regions has allowed considerable development of coastal settlement and the two villages of Sharm-el-Sheikh and Hurghada have become real little towns which offer all that a tourist may desire

in order to enjoy a pleasant and relaxed holiday without having to forego the comforts offered by more famous international tourist destinations. The sea itself has much to offer: warm clean water and an explosion of life and colour right from depths of a few metres. Mask, snorkel and a pair

of fins suffice in order to enjoy the incredible teeming life in this sea, whilst an underwater diving certification which can be obtained on the spot in a few days unlocks the door to all that lives in greater depths. The sight of such

a profusion of life stimulates the curiousity and makes one wish to increase one's knowledge and understanding of the behaviour and habits of all the strange

inhabitants of this underwater Eden, whether fish, crustaceans, turtles, shells or dolphins. This book intends to satisfy this desire, providing the enthusiast with a practical guide to Red Sea fauna and allowing him to identify the more common species. To facilitate this recognition, every species is illustrated with one or more photographs, all taken underwater of living subjects, and

these are accompanied by a simple but scientifically correct text which describes the particular characteristics of each group. Each photograph is provided with the Latin name of the species which, though it may seem unnecessarily complicated, is actually the only official language of science.

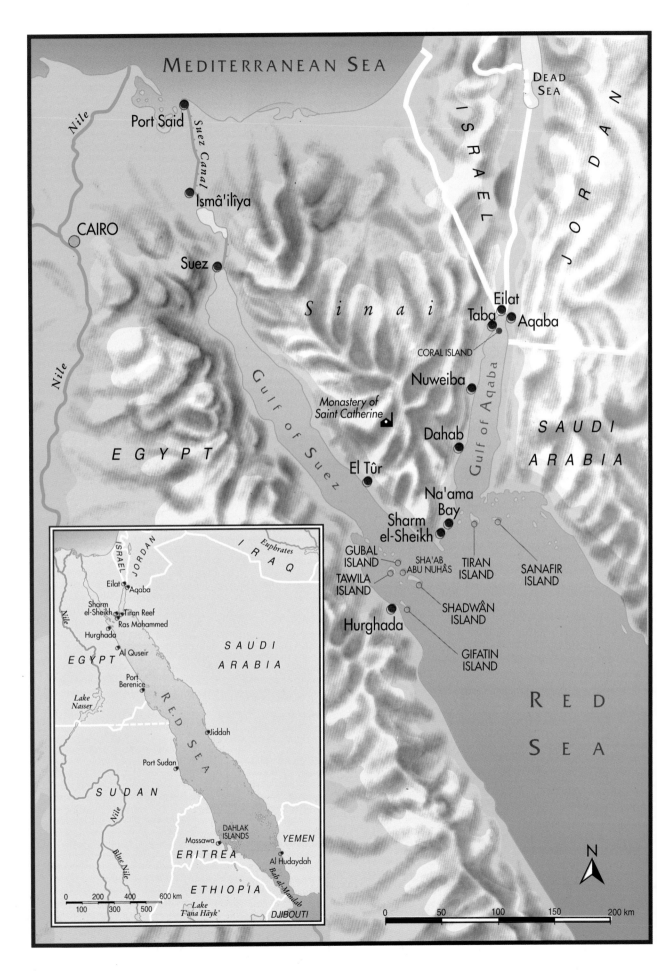

MEDITERRANEAN SEA

Nile

Port Said

Suez Canal

Ismâ'ilîya

CAIRO

Suez

DEAD SEA

ISRAEL

JORDAN

S i n a i

Nile

Eilat
Taba
Aqaba

CORAL ISLAND

Nuweiba

Monastery of
Saint Catherine

Gulf of Suez

Gulf of Aqaba

Dahab

SAUDI
ARABIA

EGYPT

El Tûr

Na'ama
Bay

Sharm
el-Sheikh

GUBAL
ISLAND

SHA'AB
ABU NUHÂS

TIRAN
ISLAND

SANAFIR
ISLAND

TAWILA
ISLAND

SHADWÂN
ISLAND

Hurghada

GIFATIN
ISLAND

R E D

S E A

N

Inset map

ISRAEL
JORDAN
IRAQ

Euphrates

Eilat
Aqaba

Sharm
el-Sheikh
Tiran Reef

Ras Mohammed

Nile

Hurghada

EGYPT

Al Quseir

SAUDI
ARABIA

Port
Berenice

Lake
Nasser

R E D   S E A

Jiddah

Port Sudan

SUDAN

Nile

DAHLAK
ISLANDS

Massawa

ERITREA

YEMEN

Al Hudaydah

Blue Nile

ETHIOPIA

Lake
T'ana Hāyk'

DJIBOUTI

Bab al-Mandab

0   200   400   600 km
  100   300   500

0   50   100   150   200 km

4

THE RED SEA

The Red Sea, having a length of 2350 kilometres and a width of 350 km. at its widest point (on a level with Eritrea), is like a long tube joining the Mediterranean Sea to the Indian Ocean. From a geological point of view it lies right in one of the danger zones of the planet, on the long fault which stretches from the great lakes of central-east Africa as far as the Gulf of Aqaba and the Jordan valley. Despite the fact that it is so narrow, it is therefore, a very deep sea, reaching almost 3000 metres in the central area and dropping 600-800 metres in many points near the reef: a wall of water on which scuba divers who venture to the reef's external drops find themselves swimming. On the other hand, the northernmost end, near the Gulf of Suez and the southernmost end near the Bab al Mandab straits are much shallower with depths not over 60 metres in the first case and 100 metres in the second. Even through it is linked to the Indian Ocean, the Red Sea can be regarded as a closed sea, and even its fauna, considered biologically as belonging to the Indo-Pacific region, boasts 20% endemic species. Although the fauna is more or less the same throughout the Red Sea, the characteristics of the seabottom vary greatly. The **Gulf of Aqaba** is very deep, reaching 1600 metres in places, but its coasts are sandy with coral formations which are not exceptionally luxuriant in the northernmost part but become gradually richer as one moves south. The end of the **Sinai** peninsula is one of the most beautiful areas in the whole of the Red Sea and **Ras Mohammad**, the extreme tip is classed among the ten most beautiful diving zones in the world. Nearby lies **Sharm-el-Sheikh**, a little fishing village which has developed into a well-equipped tourist resort and is still in a state of continual expansion, besieged by divers from all over the world, particularly Europeans. Everyday several hundred divers dive in these waters and recently steps have been taken to regulate certain areas with the creation of the Ras Mohammad marine park in order to avoid excessive human presence damaging the delicate marine ecosystem. **Hurghada**, on the Egyptian shores of the Red Sea, has also experienced an exceptional tourist boom in the last few years. The seabottom, however, is still very beautiful and it is to be hoped that it will not suffer excessive damage in the years to come. Venturing further south the adventurous Red Sea begins. There are no more hotels, restaurants, div-

The Dahlak Islands, a swim in the turquoise waters of Mojeidi, the easternmost island

Zabargad, the southern side of the island with its beautiful lagoon

ing structures and equipment shops. The shores are deserted, with a few small local settlements, and are often under military control which prohibits transit along the coast road and landing on the beaches. Only a few chartered boats equipped for diving safaris venture into these waters which are naturally much less visited and are semi-virgin. The **Brothers Islands** are situated slightly offshore, and south of these lies **Dedalus reef**; these are considered real paradises for diving. Nearer the shore rises the mythic little island of **Zabargad**, called *Topazos* in ancient times, with its old olivine mines, which were mined right from the XVIIIth Egyptian dynasty. Here the seabottom has a very unusual appearance, having a series of coral pinnacles which rise up from the sea bed towards the surface like monolythic rocks. This is the kingdom of fire coral and Alcyonarian soft corals, which thrive in few places as they do here.

Over the boundary with Sudan, one finds oneself in an area which in the 1980s experienced a certain amount of diving tourism thanks to the presence of a little fleet of Italian charter boats at **Port Sudan**. However, tourism in these areas is now much diminished due to the political instability of the country and the difficulty with flight connections. This is a great pity because the Sudanese waters are possibly the most beautiful in the Red Sea and are certainly the most wild. Every trip to the Sudan has the aura of adventure and every dive the thrill of meeting sharks and large pelagics. The Sudanese reefs rise like mushrooms from the always considerable depths and because of this are beautiful and real havens of life.

Still further south in Eritrea are the **Dahlaks**, a hundred or so islands, which are remembered with affection by all old Italian divers because it was to here that the first mythic Italian diving expedition to the Red Sea set out in now-long-ago 1953, aboard the motorship *Formica*. Names like Quilici, Vailati, Roghi and Bucher took part in this expedition, along with many others who have now become legendary. The seabottom here, however, is not among the most beautiful, having a relatively modest madreporic development and drops which soon end on sand, all in water which is not very limpid due to the enormous development of plankton. The fauna is, on the other hand, very rich and the opportunity for exciting encounters is guaranteed.

Finally there are the turbulent straits of **Bab al Mandab** and the waters of the **Seven Brothers**, a little archipelago in the middle of currents and tides. Although exceptionally rich in fish, the water is not as limpid as it might be and the tourist structures leave much to be desired. The east coasts are, on the other hand, "off-limits", which is a great pity, especially regarding the northern-central Saudi ones which may be the most beautiful areas in the entire Red Sea. We can think of them as a nature reserve for future divers, hoping that sooner or later they decide to open their doors to tourism.

CORAL REEFS

Normally one imagines tropical seas as being rich in life, but in actual fact the warm and transparent waters of the tropics are very poor in nutritious substances and thus are under populated by fish and other organisms. A coral reef is, on the other hand, an explosion of life, with a large number of animal and plant species continually competing for space, which makes it an extremely rich and complex environment. To express it in an analogue in dry land terms, one could call it an oasis in a large desert. The secret of such thriving luxuriant life lies in the particular biology of the hard corals, also called coral builders, animals that generally form colonies. These organisms are able to extract calcium carbonate from the water, with which they make their skeleton. On top of this other calcareous layers are laid down, forming over a few million years, the great coral formations. Single colonies can reach huge dimensions, weighing dozens of tons, with a volume that would fill the living room of a normal apartment.

One of the most striking aspects of the corals is the incredible variety of shapes that they can form: spherical, pillar-shaped, fan-shaped or branched. Furthermore, the external morphology of the same species may be more delicate or solid depending on whether it grows in calm or rough waters.

They also show great variety in colour, with shades of yellow and pink, green and purple, brown and blue.

The colouring lasts as long as the corals are living; after their death they loose the surface tissue and only the white calcareous skeletons, covered with little holes where the polyps lived remain. These are the living part of the great colonies. Each single polyp looks like a little contractile sac with an annular crown of tentacles arranged round an opening which acts as a mouth. The tentacles have stinging cells which eject a filament similar to an arrow and a toxin capable of stunning small prey like the microscopic shell fish on which the polyps feed. Most of the species hunt by night, while during the day the polyps remain retracted in their holes.

An important characteristic of the corals which build large reefs is the presence of particular unicellular algae which live inside their tissues. Although the precise details of the workings of this unusual relationship based on a mutual exchange of favours are not yet entirely clear, it is known for certain that these algae aid the depostion of calcium carbonate for the construction of the corals, that they remove waste substances produced by the polyps, turning them into other substances which are useful to the colonies, and that they also produce oxygen in greater quanties than is consumed. The proof of the importance of these minute plants is that the corals that are without them only form colonies of a modest size.

Other organisms able to secrete calcareous substances, like "fire corals" and many species of "coral-algae" which are all-important in the building of the coral formations due to their cementing function, contribute to the construction of the reefs. The great coral reefs are usually to be found in shallow waters, only rarely as deep as 100 metres, to allow the algae in them the necessary light to photo-synthesise. Furthermore, the corals require warm water (between 20° and 35°), and cannot tolerate low salinity or very turbid waters.

Typical appearance of a coral reef

When on the subject of the dangers of tropical seas, one's thoughts race straight to **Sharks** (a), almost as if they have no other purpose in life but to lie in wait for the next tourist in order to attack him and satisfy their terrible voracity. Nothing is further from the truth. There are sharks, and in certain areas they may also be quite numerous, but they are not at all the satanic beasts that we generally believe them to be. Photographers know this well, as they have great problems getting near enough to a shark for a "photographic shot"; at the slightest attempt to approach them they swim away. The species which really are dangerous are few and sightings are rare, but even if they are encountered, an attack is by no means certain and is, in fact, rather improbable. Despite this one must not forget that sharks are powerful predators at the apex of the food chain, with an extremely efficient physical structure and that they are remarkably skillful in attacking. Thus, all risky behaviour should be avoided, like swimming on the surface of the water rotating arms and kicking legs (similar to a wounded fish), bathing in harbours and in turbid water, hunting with a spear-gun (vibrations and blood attract and excite sharks), diving at night in places where shark presence is known, and trying to attract them by offering food. If one approaches you, do not try to escape: face the animal, perhaps moving towards it and constantly maintain a calm demeanour. Other seemingly to-be-feared fish are inoffensive in reality if they are not interfered with or wounded. Among these are **Moray eels** (d) (*Muraenidae*), some of which grow to a phenomenal size, but which are, despite their reputation, timid and wary. Or **Barracudas** (b) with their threatening appearance and terrible teeth, which sometimes group together in shoals of several hundred and come very close to divers

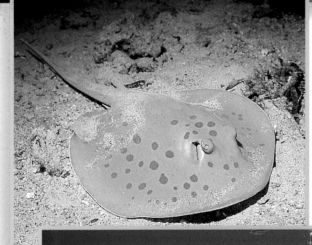

ANIMALS

without, however, attacking them. **Trigger-fish** (f) may bite, on the other hand, particularly the *Balistoides viridescens*, when it is guarding its eggs which are laid in large circular nests. If one goes too near, it does not hestitate for a moment, but attacks and one must beat a hasty retreat to avoid its couragious and determined action. However the real danger of the tropics lies not in animals that bite, but in poisonous stings or contact with stinging sea life. The greatest risk is posed by the *Scorpaenidae* which are furnished with spines connected to poison-glands for defense, situated on the dorsal, ventral and anal fins.

Some *Scorpaenidae*, like the **Lionfish** (e) (*Pterois*) are easily recognisable because of the striking richness and brightness of their colouring which warns possible "troublemakers" of their efficient means of defense. Others, like the much feared **Stonefish** (h) (*Synanceia verrucosa*) or the large **Scorpionfishes** (*Scorpaenopsis barbatus and S. diabolus*) lie on the bottom of the sea, perfectly camouflaged and immobile waiting for prey to come within their striking range. If they are trodden on by mistake or touched, they may sting, injecting a terrible poison which causes unbearable shooting pains and local swelling, followed by profuse sweating, respiratory problems, quickening of heart beat, high fever and, in some cases, partial paralysis. Pain can continue for several days and in some cases the sting may cause death. The poisonous substances used by the *Scorpaenidae* are neurotoxins which are destroyed by heat (thermolabile), therefore the part of the body in question must be immersed in hot water, as hot as is bearable and diluted oxidising agents, like potassium permanganate must be applied to fight the toxic effect of the poison; analeptics for the heart and adrenaline and cortisone must also be administered. Another bottom-dwelling fish, which partially covers itself with sand is the **Stingray** (c), which is ubiquitous in the Red Sea, particularly the spotted species (*Taeniura lymma*) which has a spine connected to a poison-gland. It seldom uses it, only if it is trodden on or interfered with, but if stung, the wound is very painful and can result in infection and gangrene in the limb involved. The **Electric Ray** (g) is of a simi-

i

l

m

n

lar shape and also inhabits sandy seabottoms where it covers itself completely with sand. It does not have spines; instead it possesses an efficient electric system able to give a strong electric shock to whoever dares to annoy it. A sting which in rare cases has shown itself to be lethal is that of certain beautiful **Cone-shells** (m), for example the *Conus textile*. These molluscs have a sophisticated poison-apparatus that they use to paralyse their prey. They can discharge real little harpoons, injecting a powerful toxin. They are mostly to be seen at night and are harmless as long as they are not picked up. **Sea urchins** are well-known for the unpleasant results if they come into contact with hands or feet. They come out of their shelters in the reef at night and stud whole stretches of seabottom. The **diadem sea urchins** (o) have long, fine black spines which easily penetrate flesh, breaking off and causing painful "wounds" because of the toxins contained in the thin epidermic layer which covers the spines. Another sea urchin to avoid is *Asthenosoma varium* (i). This species has the points of its short red spines covered with minute white vesicles full of poison. When the spines pen-

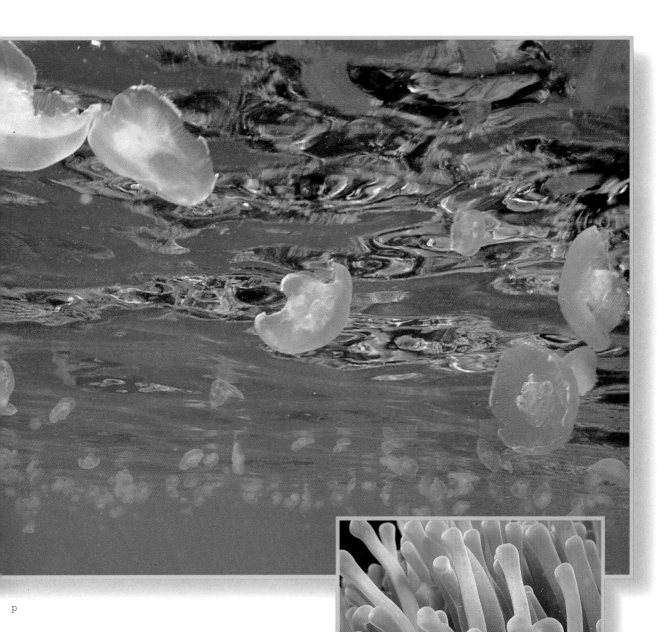

p

etrate the victim's skin, the vesicles break open and release their poison, causing immediate and intense pain. Many organisms sting if they come into contact with the skin and it is easy to protect oneself from them by wearing a wet-suit complete with footwear and a pair of gloves. First of all there is the extremely common **Fire Coral** (l) (*Millepora* species), a hydrozoa of a form similar to branching or fan-shaped corals, which is of a browny-yellow ochre colour with whitish tips. Its great power to sting is due to it possessing small organs (nematocysts) in surface cells which eject poisoned threads containing a powerful toxin able to inflict painful "burns". If one does touch one of these corals, the burn must be rinsed profusely with sea water, rubbing energetically, and then alluminium sulphate or a cortisone cream must be applied. Some types of **Jellyfish** (n, p), **Sea Anemones** (q) and other **Cnidaria** are just as bad for stings, but it is easy to protect oneself against these by wearing the normal clothing used by divers.

q

SNORKELLING AND SCUBA

The Red Sea is one of the areas which lends itself best to exploration equipped simply with fins, mask and snorkel, an activity known today by the name of snorkelling.

Its seabottom is, in fact, characterised by reefs which emerge from the water, or are semi-submerged, allowing tranquil and complete observation of this extremely rich environment and its inhabitants even to those who limit themselves to swimming on the surface. The first few metres of the reef are the richest in life and colour, a megalopolis where a large part of the fish and animals of this sea are concentrated. Small descents of only a few metres holding one's breath enable one to discover the inhabitants of the caves and sandy bottom, whilst a swim in deeper waters may provide exciting surprises like encounters with large pelagics and predators like barracudas and sharks which are easier to approach like this than when scuba diving for the very reason that a snorkeller is more silent.

Very little equipment is necessary: a good mask which is securely watertight, a not excessively long snorkel of quite large diameter and a pair of fins. On this subject it is worth stopping a moment to examine the numerous different models: open or closed shoe, long or short, with or without special slits for the passage of water or other devices to aid propulsion.

The best fins for snorkelling are those with a closed shoe which are not excessively long or rigid, even if this depends on individual musculature and practice. Open shoe fins allow, on the other hand, the use of boots, with a strong rubber sole which are ideal for walking in shallow water and on the reef, but tend to make one's feet float, rendering swimming less efficient.

Precious advice for snorkellers is to wear a complete protective garment, composed of jacket and trousers which protect the body from contact with corals and with the many stinging animals. These garments are available on the market both in neoprene from 2 or 3 mm thickness and in lycra. The first offers good protection from the cold as well, but requires a few kilos of weights to cancel out the positive buoyancy thrust. The second does not require this, but offers reduced thermal protection. Hands should also be protected with a pair of cloth or leather gloves, even if it is a good rule never to touch the reef, both in order not to damage it, and also so as to avoid inadvertently touching scorpionaeds and other dangerous sea life.

Scuba diving opens the doors to a marvellous world which is still largely uncontaminated and nowadays it is so easy and within the reach of everyone that anyone who is at all used swimming should try the thrill of it. In the most famous centres in the northern part of the Red Sea there are a great many schools and Diving Centres which teach the basic rules of diving and issue the relevant international certification in less than a week. But it is better still to obtain this certification in one's own country so as to be ready for autonomous diving from the very first day on the Red Sea.

Those who already have this certification normally possess their own equipment which it is worth bringing with them because of the great cost of hiring it and the fact that equipment is not always readily available on site, and finally because well checked and tested personal equipment guarantees far greater safety.

As general advice on equipment, remember that the taps and fittings of the compressed-air cylinders are almost always single attachment, thus it is useless to bring two separate regulators when only one of them can be mounted on the cylinder; instead it is necessary to form an "octopus" mounting two second stages on a single first stage. The wet-suit must be complete (jacket with long sleeves and full length trousers) in order to avoid abrasions on the reef. As to the thickness of the neoprene, it depends on the season and the latitude. Whilst in the Sudan and the southern Red Sea, a 3 mm wet-suit may be sufficient all year round, in the northern part of the Red Sea, from December to April, it is advisable to choose a 5 mm hooded model.

The best boots for scuba use are those with rigid soles which require open-heel fins. An equalizing jacket is obligatory: this is the one piece of equipment which more than any other has, for the general public, opened the door to diving. A good pair of gloves, a knife, a torch with batteries, control instruments and a few spare parts for the equipment must not be forgotten given that only in the more important centres on the Red Sea is there good equipment availability, whilst in the more isolated places, virtually nothing can be found.

UNDERWATER PHOTOGRAPHY

Whoever dives in the thriving and exuberant waters of a tropical sea is unlikely to resist for long the desire to take home a visible reminder of it in the form of photographs. Any type of equipment could be suitable for this purpose, even if in order to obtain the best results the more sophisticated and expensive apparatus is necessary, whilst the more simple and economical equipment, like the recent "use and throw" cameras are only fit for souvenir photographs of unexceptional quality.

The camera which has been universally used by underwater photographers throughout the world for the last thirty years is the Nikonos, which was designed as an amphibious camera and can be taken underwater as it is without requiring a watertight housing. By now it is in it's fifth model series and has interchangeable lenses (out of water!) and a good range of lenses, going from an extreme wide-angle lens to a small telephoto lens. The current model is also provided with automatic exposure which greatly helps the photographer in the not always easy search for the correct exposure.

The alternative to the Nikonos is the old-fashioned, but still valid, possibility of enclosing a dry land camera in a watertight case. The cameras used in this case are reflex monolens cameras which offer perfect vision and focus through the reflex viewfinder and which from this point of view are much superior to the Nikonos.

In all cases an important feature to look for when choosing an underwater camera is the possibility of lens interchange, given that a general lens does not exist and every photographic situation and every subject requires the right lens. The "standard" lens of the Nikonos is 35 mm which allows the photography of fish, sponges, starfish, soft corals, large crustaceans and head and shoulders portraits of divers. The 28 mm is, on the other hand, suitable for slightly larger subjects and allows one to take photographs nearer the subject. The 20 mm is already a quite powerful wide-angle lens and thus is suitable for portraits of divers and large sea animals, shoals of fish, gorgonians and large portions of reef. The mythic 15 mm is, finally, the strongest wide-angle lens in the Nikonos outfit and is used to photograph larger subjects, like wrecks, to portray the reef environment, for portraits of divers from nearby and for large throngs of fish photographed close to. It is a lens with great depth of field, which manages to correct errors in focusing well, but which is not suitable for photographing fish and other subjects of a small size which would appear tiny in the picture.

These Nikonos lenses correspond respectively to 50-35-26-20 mm mounted on a housed reflex camera provided with a dome port. Furthermore, with a housed reflex camera macro lenses from 50 and 100 mm which are ideal for photographing small sized subjects or animals which are difficult to approach, can be used.

Even if one is taking photographs in the first few metres, the use of an electronic strobe is indispensable, not so much to light up the surroundings as to revive the colours which are filtered and absorbed by the water. Without a flash all underwater photographs would have a bluish monochrome tone; this would be a great pity in a world which is so rich in warm and intense colours. Dozens of models with different prices and characteristics are available on the market, and, absurdly, they can cost much more than the camera itself.

If one is fascinated by the heterogeneous underwater microcosm, one must procure a series of extension tubes or additional lenses for the Nikonos or a macro lens for those using a housed reflex camera. Contrary to what one might imagine, macro is easier than scene photography and the first real photographic satisfaction will often come from taking pictures of the smallest inhabitants of the reef.

As far as films go there is no choice, reverse-type films, better known as slides, are compulsory. The negative films which provide colour prints, give poor chromatic results due to the difficult and incorrect interpretation of underwater colours by automatic printers. As far as sensitivity goes, films from 50-100 ISO are preferable to more sensitive films, in order to obtain a more definite and clear-cut image.

On page 12, a group of scuba divers on their way to a diving site in Sudan

Nikonos V is the only amphibious camera with interchangeable lenses and is the most used in underwater photography

On page 14, a diver underwater with a large gorgonian in the foreground

A wreck appearing on the surface in the straits of Tiran

One of the Fiat 1100s in the hold of the "Umbria", the most famous wreck in the Red Sea, voluntarily sunk by its captain in 1940, off Port Sudan; underwater wreck of the "Dana", sunk at Sha' ab Abu Nuhâs (northern Egypt) in the 80s

1 - Grey Reef Shark (*Carcharhinus wheeleri*)

SHARKS

Open sea/reef - diurnal/nocturnal - solitary/gregarious -
carnivorous - snorkelling/scuba - 0/70 m

The Red Sea has a very large number of sharks and in some areas, for example the open sea reefs in the Sudanese waters, it is practically impossible not to encounter at least one during a dive. They have not got a very good reputation, but with the gradual abandonment of underwater fishing and the spread of scuba diving it has been discovered that sharks are, all considered, peaceful and timid fish. Thus we should not feel worried when we see them underwater and it will soon become clear, on the contrary, that it is very difficult to come near enough them to take a photograph. The species which are potentially dangerous to man are few and to meet them is very rare and entirely a matter of chance.

All sharks are cartilaginous fishes and are thus related to rays, manta rays, eagle rays and electric rays.

One of the sharks which one is most likely to encounter when scuba diving or snorkelling is the Whitetip Reef Shark *(Triaenodon obesus)*, of elongate form and with the dorsal and tail fins tipped with white. Sometimes one sees it resting on the seabottom or inside caves, completely immobile.

The Grey Reef Shark *(Carcharhinus wheeleri)* approachs along the reef slopes. It can reach 175 cm

2 - Whitetip Reef Shark *(Triaenodon obesus)*
3 - Silvertip Shark *(Carcharhinus albimarginatus)*
4, 5 - Scalloped Hammerhead Shark *(Sphyrna lewinii)*

in length and can be recognised by a lighter strip on the dorsal fin, whilst the tail is edged with black. Similar to the Grey Reef Shark, but with all its fins edged with white is the Silvertip Shark *(Carcharhinus albimarginatus)* which can grow to 180 cm and may behave in a rather territorial fashion, making forays against the diver in order to drive him out of its territory.
An encounter with the Scalloped Hammerhead Shark *(Sphyrna lewinii)* is always exciting. Often they group together in shoals of a great number and can be recognised by the characteristic form of the head. They are considered potentially dangerous, but in reality have never bothered divers.

7

6, 7 - Spotted Reef Stingray (*Taeniura lymma*)
8 - The dangerous spine of a Spotted Reef Stingray

8

Dasyatididae (Stingrays) - Myliobatidae (Eagle Rays) - Mobulidae (Manta Rays and Sea devils) - Torpedinidae (Electric Rays)

Stingrays possess a cartilaginous skeleton like sharks, and have a flattened body with a long tail armed with a venomous spine. They are bottom-living fish, resting on the sandy seabottom partially covered with sediment and they feed on molluscs, crustaceans and little fishes which they manage to hunt out even if they are totally hidden in the sand thanks to a sophisticated reception system that allows them to perceive the weak electric field produced by a living organism. The Spotted Reef Stingray *(Taeniura lymma)* which has a beautiful ochre yellow livery, spotted with blue marks is very widespread in the Red Sea.

9

9 - Manta Ray *(Manta birostris)*
10 - Spotted Eagle Ray *(Aetobatis narinari)*
11 - Electric Ray *(Torpedo sinuspersici)*

10

11

Eagle Rays *(Aetobatis narinari)* swim in the middle water and are distinguished by their marbled skin and their long whip-like tail which also is armed with a venomous spine. They swim with great elegance, moving their "wings" (which in reality are fins) like large birds.

The enormous and completely harmless Manta Rays are also master swimmers, swimming in perpetual movement and feeding on plankton. They can reach a colossal size, even up to 6 or 7 metres "wing" span. In some periods of the year, especially in the southern part of the Red Sea, they gather in huge throngs, probably for the purpose of reproduction.

Electric rays are, on the other hand, benthonic, that is they are bottom-dwellers and the front half of their body is rounded. They possess an unusual and very effective method of capturing their prey: an electric shock, produced by organs which are similar to rechargeable batteries.

Sphyraenoidea - Barracuda

Open sea - diurnal/nocturnal - solitary/gregarious -
carnivorous - snorkelling/scuba - 0/50 m

An encounter with a large shoal of young barracudas swimming in the middle water is always exciting. They look like ferocious predators with their jaws half open and their terrible teeth visible. All members of this family are voracious predators, but as long as they are not annoyed or provoked they avoid attacking humans. In order to attract them one must take a shiny object (metal or similar) underwater and they will approach, their curiosity aroused.

The "giant" of the group is the *Sphyraena barracuda*, a fish which can reach over 2 metres in length and 40 kg in weight. When adult it is a solitary animal, mainly active in the daytime and may be encountered everywhere from the waters of harbours to the open sea.

It is held to be the sole member of the family responsible for attacks on man, all of which have taken place in dark and turbid water where it is easy to mistake a human limb for prey.

12 - Great barracuda (*Sphyraena barracuda*)
13 - Shoals of barracudas (*Sphyraena sp.*)

14

15

Carangidae - Trevally

Open sea - diurnal - solitary/gregarious - carnivorous - snorkelling/scuba - 0/60 m

These exceptional swimmers of perfect hydrodynamic form with beautiful silvery colours are occasional visitors to the reef. They move from the open sea to the shallow waters and often swim in large shoals when they are young fish, becoming solitary when they have reached a large size.
They are all carnivores and their prey is made up of molluscs, fish and crustaceans. Large Trevally appear as if by magic at the flapping of a wounded fish. This is one of the most exciting encounters for divers.

14, 16 - Bigeye Trevally (*Caranx sexfasciatus*)
15 - Bluefin Trevally (*Caranx melampygus*)

16

Ephippidae - Platax or Batfish

Open sea - diurnal - solitary/gregarious - carnivorous - snorkelling/scuba - 0/25 m

The body of the *Platax* or Batfish is laterally much compressed and of a circular form, so much so as to call to mind a plate or a frying pan. They are covered with shiny silver-coloured scales with dark stripes and are not great swimmers. They owe their name of batfish to the great growth that the dorsal and ventral fins undergo at a youthful age, making them look like wings. They swim in the middle water in compact groups going to the seabottom from time to time to capture large invertebrates.

17

17 - Longfin Batfish (*Platax teira*)
18 - Circular Batfish
    (*Platax orbicularis*)

18

Lutianidae - Snappers

Open sea/reef - solitary/gregarious -
diurnal/nocturnal - carnivorous -
snorkelling/scuba - 5/100 m

Some of the most important
tropical species from a commercial point of view, due to the
quality of their flesh are to be
found in this group.

Most of these fish live either
alone or in little groups near the
reef in shallow or intermediate
depths of water (up to 100 m),
though some species can reach
500 m. depth.

They feed on a wide range of
organisms, all animal, which
they capture prevalently at night.
They are long-living fish which
can reach the venerable old-age
of 21. The Twinspot Snapper
(*Lutjanus bohar*) can grow to 1
metre long and is one of the
great predators of the reef.

19 - Twinspot Snapper
    (*Lutjanus bohar*)
20, 22 - Bluestripe Snapper
    (*Lutjanus kasmira*)

Caesionidae - Fusiliers

Pelagic - diurnal - gregarious - carnivorous - snorkelling/scuba - 5/60m

Comparing these fish with the *Lutianidae* to which they have a similiar appearance, they are thinner and more elongate. They form large shoals and feed, during the day on the small animal organisms which live in the middle water above the coral reef. An encounter with *Caesionidae* is very likely on the edge of the external slopes of the reef, and it is always thrilling for the diver who finds himself enveloped in clouds of fishes.

21, 23 - Fusiliers (*Caesio sp.*)

21

23

Muraenidae - Morays

Reef - diurnal/nocturnal - solitary - carnivorous - snorkelling/scuba - 2/50 m

Morays are particularly well suited to the coral reef environment: their elongate and strongly muscular form and smooth scaleless skin allow them to slip into narrow holes with the greatest of ease.

Their snake-like appearance, their sometimes remarkable size (up to 3 metres) and the continual opening and closing of the mouth (a motion connected with breathing) inspire a certain fear. But in actual fact they are not at all dangerous for man, if not provoked or annoyed; on the contrary, they are rather timid. However, just the same, one must never put one's hand into their holes, as bites are extremly painful and dangerous due to the moray's sharp teeth which are turned towards the inside of the mouth. Morays undergo a sex change during growth, changing from male to female.

24, 26 - Giant Moray (*Gymnothorax javanicus*)
25 - Grey Moray (*Siderea grisea*)

24

26

25

Anthiidae - Anthias

Reef - diurnal - gregarious - carnivorous - snorkelling/scuba - 0/15 m

These fish are a few centimetres long, of a brilliant reddish orange and populate every point of the reef in very large numbers.

They live near the coral formations, hunting little plankton organisms during the day. They pass the night, on the other hand, carefully hidden away in cracks and small holes.

The colouring and appearance of the males is different from that of the females and a precise ratio between the two sexes exists in every group: usually one male to ten females. The curious sex change phenomenon sees to it that if the male dies or disappears, one of the adult females from the same group takes his place, changing sex and livery.

29

27, 31 - Scalefin Anthias male (*Anthias squamipinnis*)
28 - Scalefin Anthias female (*Anthias squamipinnis*)
29 - Scalefin Anthias male (*Anthias taeniatus*)
30 - A shoal of Scalefin Anthias (*Anthias squamipinnis*)

30

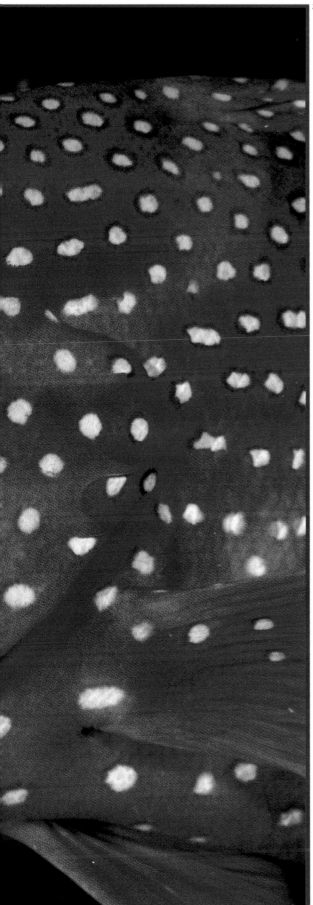

Serranidae - Groupers

Reef - diurnal/nocturnal - solitary -carnivorous -
snorkelling/scuba - 5/200 m

Groupers are widespread in tropical seas from a
few metres to over 200 metres depth and are famous for their high commercial value. Large sharp
canines are a feature in most of the species and
testify to the fearsome nature of these predators
who mainly feed on fish and crustaceans.

These fish undergo sex changes in the same way
as the *Anthiidae*, with the difference that in this
group there are also species characterised by
"synchronous hermaphroditism", that is, they possess functioning male and female sex organs all
their life. The largest examples, which can weigh
dozens of kilos, appear to be very long lived. They
are powerful predators, markedly territorial, and
are positioned at the top of the food chain, therefore killing them may result in a distinct unbalance
in the ecosystem of the reef.

32, 33 - Coral Grouper (*Cephalopholis miniata*)

34, 35 - Coral Grouper (*Cephalopholis miniata*)
36 - Lunartail Grouper (*Variola louti*)

37 - Halfspotted Grouper (*Cephalopholis hemistiktos*)
38, 40 - Blacktip Grouper (*Epinephelus fasciatus*)
39 - Roving Grouper (*Plectropomus maculatus*)

41 - Roving Grouper (*Plectropomus maculatus*)
42 - Greasy Grouper (*Epinephelus tauvina*)
43 - Peacock Grouper (*Cephalopholis argus*)
44 - Summana Grouper (*Epinephelus summana*)

Haemulidae - Grunts

Reef - diurnal/nocturnal - gregarious - carnivorous - snorkelling/scuba - 2/40 m

The name of this fish comes from the strange sounds that it emits gnashing its teeth and amplifying the sound with its swimbladder. These fish are mostly active during the night, which they pass hunting invertebrates on the sea bottom. During the day they swim slowly round the madreporic formations often in very large groups. A dramatic change in colouring with growth is characteristic in many species, but is not accompanied by sex change.

45, 46 - Blackspotted Grunt (*Plectorhynchus gaterinus*)   45

46

Labridae - Wrasses

Reef - diurnal - solitary - carnivorous -
snorkelling/scuba - 0/50 m

The family of Wrasses is second only to the *Gobiidae* in number of species. Its members vary enormously in form, colour and size, going from fish a few centimetres long to colossi of 2 metres. Many species of this family possess strong teeth which protude from their mouth and which they use to chop up sea urchins, crustaceans and molluscs.

Most of the *Labridae* are brightly coloured, the livery changing from young to adult (with intermediate phases) and according to sex. The sex change phenomenon is very widespread in this family where individuals reach sexual maturity as females but may, however, change into males in the course of their life.

The Wrasses are typically diurnal fish. In fact they are the first fish to "retire" at dusk, lying on the seabottom or protected in a crevice, and they are among the last to resume activity the following morning.

When they swim among the madrepores they only use the pectoral fins, resorting to the caudal (tail) fins solely in the case of sudden flight or pursuit. A curious member of this family which merits particular attention is the Cleaner Wrasse.

47 - Slingjaw Wrasse, male (*Epibulus insidiator*)
48 - Cleaner Wrasse (*Labroides dimidiatus*)
49 - Slingjaw Wrasse, female (*Epibulus insidiator*)
50 - Checkerboard Wrasse (*Halichoeres hortulanus*)

51 - Bandcheek Wrasse
  (*Cheilinus digrammus*)
52 - Redbreasted Wrasse
  (*Cheilinus fasciatus*)

53 - Lyretail Hogfish, juvenile
  (*Bodianus anthioides*)
54 - Thicklip Wrasse
  (*Hemigymnus melapterus*)
55 - Klunzinger's Wrasse
  (*Thalassoma klunzingeri*)

53

54

CLEANER WRASSE

The Cleaner Wrasse (La-broides dimidiatus) has chosen an unusual method of procuring food: it cleans other fish of parasites, dead scales and pieces of skin. The fish are very willing to submit to this service, given that they have no other means of freeing themselves from these bothersome guests. The Cleaners organise real cleaning stations, rather like a car wash, with fish patiently waiting, and the fortunate fish whose turn it is with mouth and gills wide open and an agile Cleaner darting round him, slipping into every opening. To attract "clients" the cleaner performs a kind of mimetic dance, the meaning of which appears to be quite clear to whoever is in need of a toilette.

55

56

57

58

59

60

61

62

63

44

56 - Diana's Hogfish (*Bodianus diana*)
57 - Axilspot Hogfish, juvenile (*Bodianus axillaris*)
58 - Chiseltooth Wrasse (*Pseudodax moluccanus*)
59 - Clown Coris, juvenile (*Coris aygula*)
60 - Clown Coris, intermediate (*Coris aygula*)
61 - Clown Coris, adult male (*Coris aygula*)
62, 63 - Moon Wrasse (*Thalassoma lunare*)
64 - Napoleonfish (*Cheilinus undulatus*)

65

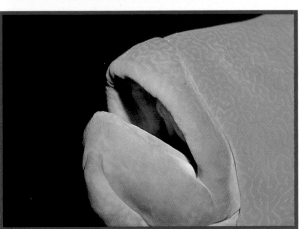

66

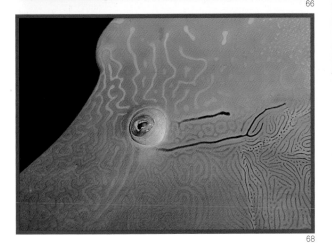

68

67

46

65/67, 69, 70 - Napoleonfish (*Cheilinus undulatus*)
68 - Adult Napoleonfish, eye with hieroglyphics
(*Cheilinus undulatus*)

NAPOLEONFISH

The Napoleonfish (Cheilinus undulatus*), which owes its name to the prominent lump on its head which calls to mind the headgear of Emperor Napoleon, is one of the fish most loved by scuba divers, maybe due to its ungainly appearance, its considerable size or its expressive eye which examines one attentively. They are especially numerous at Ras Mohammad, the extreme point of Sinai, where they used to be fed with hard-boiled eggs by divers; a practice which is now justly banned. Like other Wrasses, it has a remarkable jaw articulation and can protrude its lips out of all proportion, swallowing its prey whole with a powerful suction. Young fish have a yellowy-light greyish livery, whilst the large fish boast a very elegant livery with green and blue reflections and a beautiful series of hieroglyphics on their heads.*

71

Pomacanthidae - Angelfish

Reef - diurnal - solitary - omnivorous -
snorkelling/scuba - 0-50 m

The *Pomacanthidae* are among the most typical
fish of the coral reef and are characterised by
beautiful and bright colours which change dramat-
ically with age. Even their sex changes with age :
female when young and male thereafter. The social system of the Angelfish is characterised by the
dominance of a male which defends a territory
(from a few square metres to over 1000, depending on the species) containing from 2-5 females. If
the male disappears, the largest and most dominant female changes sex and takes his place.
Their diet is made up of a great variety of organisms, both plant and animal, depending on the
species. Some *Pomacanthidae*, especially in their
juvenile period, can change occasionally into
cleaner-fish, freeing other fish from irritating parasites. They are easy to distinguish from the
Chaetodontidae as they have a pre-opercular
spine.

72

71, 75 - Emperor Angelfish (*Pomacanthus imperator*)
72 - Emperor Angelfish, juvenile (*Pomacanthus imperator*)
73 - Royal Angelfish (*Pygoplites diacanthus*)
74 - Arabian Angelfish (*Pomacanthus asfur*)
76 - Yellowbar Angelfish (*Pomacanthus maculosus*)
77 - Yellowbar Angelfish, juvenile
      (*Pomacanthus maculosus*)

73

74

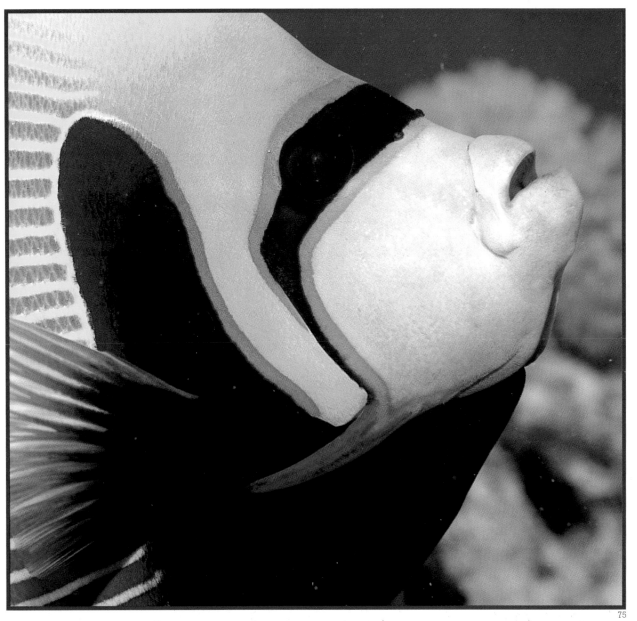

75

76   77

78

79

78, 80 - Yellowbar Angelfish
     (*Pomacanthus maculosus*)
79 - Zebra Angelfish
     (*Genicanthus caudovittatus*)

80

Chaetodontidae - Butterflyfish

Reef - diurnal - gregarious/solitary - carnivorous/omnivorous - snorkelling/scuba - 0/30 m

Butterflyfish are among the most typical and most colourful reef fish and are distinguished from the *Pomacanthidae* by the absence of the opercular spine. During the day they patrol the territory alone or in pairs, whilst they pass the night lying on the seabottom, their colouring changing slightly and becoming a bit darker. Some species feed on a vast range of organisms, others, on the other hand, specialize. Among the latter are the funny looking fishes with a long narrow face and snout that they use to eat the little polyps in the madrepores.

In most species of Butterflyfish, once couples are formed, they remain together for many years, even for their whole life.

81 - Paleface Butterflyfish
    (*Chaetodon mesoleucos*)
82 - Lined Butterflyfish
    (*Chaetodon lineolatus*)
83 - Threadfin Butterflyfish
    (*Chaetodon auriga*)

81

82

83

84

85

86

87

88

89

90

103

104

105

106

107

108

Balistidae - Triggerfish

Reef - diurnal - solitary - herbivorous/omnivorous - snorkelling/scuba - 3/50 m

The *Balistidae* are characterised by an unusual defense mechanism: a strong dorsal spine which can be locked into place by a second smaller spine. The presence of a predator or the approach of nightfall make these fish take refuge in small holes where they set off this "trigger" mechanism and thus remain stuck inside and cannot be pulled out. Most Triggerfish are solitary and diurnal. Their strong teeth allow them to eat a great variety of organisms, including certain molluscs and sea urchins which are avoided by most of the other fish. They lay their eggs in large circular nests dug in the sand and they defend them bravely, attacking whoever enters their territory, man included, without hesitation.

109

109, 110 - Orangestriped Triggerfish
    (Balistapus undulatus)
111 - Picasso Triggerfish *(Rhinecanthus assasi)*
112 - Redtooth Triggerfish *(Odonus niger)*
113, 115 - Titan Triggerfish *(Balistoides viridescens)*
114 - Blue Triggerfish *(Pseudobalistes fuscus)*

110

111

112

113

114

115

Pomacentridae - Damselfish and Clownfish

Reef - diurnal - solitary/gregarious - herbivorous/omnivorous - snorkelling/scuba - 0/25 m

The *Pomacentridae* are one of the most numerous groups in the shallow waters of the coral reef. Colouring varies greatly within the family, going from dark colours like brown, dark grey and black to bright and striking combinations of orange, yellow and electric blue.

Their diet is also very varied: some feed on plankton, others are omnivorous and eat a bit of everything - algae, small invertebrates and zooplankton. The solitary and territorial species are very brave, ready to defend their territory fearlessly even when faced with trouble much bigger than themselves.

During the mating season, the male locates a suitable space on the sea bed; he clears it and makes it orderly and then dedicates himself to an animated dance (sudden darts and extension of fins) in order to win a mate. If all goes well, the female lays eggs which are guarded with care and courage by the male until they hatch.

CLOWNFISH

To this family belong the famous clownfishes, whose name derives from the brightness of their colouring and which can only live in a relationship with large tropical sea anemones. The stinging power of the sea anemones keeps predators away from the clownfish who are able to seek refuge between their tentacles, as they are protected by their mucus. In exchange for this protection, the fish work hard to keep their host clean, freeing it from all types of residue. This is a typical case of mutualistic symbiosis, that is, when two organisms exchange reciprocal favours.

Another curious characteristic of the biology of this group concerns the sex change from male to female. A large sea anemone is usually host to a "family", made up of a couple of large fish and other smaller fish, which is governed by a rigid hierarchy. The largest and most dominant individual is the female. When it disappears, the largest adult male changes sex and takes its place, whilst another male, smaller than the former, reaches sexual maturity fast and takes on reproductive functions.

116

117

118

119

121

116 - Sulphur Damselfish (*Pomacentrus sulfureus*)
117 - Half-and-Half Chromis (*Chromis dimidiata*)
118 - Whitebelly Damselfish
    (*Amblyglyphidodon leucogaster*)
119 - Banded Dascyllus (*Dascyllus aruanus*)
120 - Sergeant Major (*Abudefduf saxatilis*)
121, 123, 125, 126 - Twobar Anemonefish
            (*Amphiprion bicinctus*)
122 - Bluegreen Chromis (*Chromis coerulea*)
124 - Domino (*Dascyllus trimaculatus*)

122

123

124

125 126

127

128

Mullidae - Mullets

Reef - diurnal - gregarious - carnivorous - snorkelling/scuba - 0/20 m

Mullets are easily recognizable due to their elongate body and a pair of long barbels located under the lower jaw. These contain chemical sense organs and are used to search for food, "rooting" in the sand. When they are not being used the barbels are withdrawn and held against the "throat" of the fish, whilst during courtship the male shakes them showily.
Mullets are all carnivorous and feed mainly on small invertebrates, even though some species do not spurn small fish.

127, 129 - Yellowsaddle Goatfish *(Parupeneus cyclostomus)*
128 - Forsskal's Goatfish *(Parupeneus forsskali)*

129

Gobiidae

Reef - diurnal - solitary/gregarious - carnivorous - snorkelling/scuba - 2/30 m

This is the most numerous fish family, numbering over 800 species spread out throughout the world. The particular elongate form of the body and the small size, no bigger than 10 cm, make them particularly suited to life near small crevices and holes where they can take refuge at the first sign of danger. Some species prefer to live in small groups among the branches of the madrepores. Some *Gobiidae* live in symbiosis with a type of shrimp (*Alpheidae* family), sharing the same shelter with them: the crustaceans make a hole in the sand and busily work to keep it free of sediment and the fish stand guard over it.

130

131

130 - Maiden Goby (*Valenciennea puellaris*)
131 - Smallscale Hover Goby (*Ptereleotris microlepis*)
132 - Magnus' Goby (*Amblyeleotris steinizi*)

132

133

Blenniidae

Reef - diurnal - solitary - herbivorous/carnivorous - snorkelling/scuba - 2/30 m

Small fish of an elongate form with a long and continuous dorsal fin, which live in the shallow waters of the reef. Despite their seemingly peaceable appearance, they are aggressive animals, ready to defend their territory bravely even against much larger beings. They can often be seen inside little holes in the madrepores into which they slip tail first, leaving only their agreeable little head with its two large eyes sticking out.

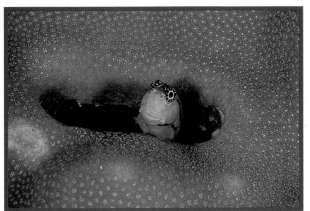

134

133 - Red Sea Mimic Blenny *(Ecsenius gravieri)*
134 - Nalolo *(Ecsenius nalolo)*
135 - Mimic Blenny *(Aspidontus taeniatus)*

135

Scorpaenidae - Scorpionfish

Benthonic - solitary - diurnal/nocturnal - carnivorous - snorkelling/scuba - 2/30 m

These fish take their name from the venomous spines positioned on the dorsal fin, which are characteristic of many species. They are typically sedentary animals and are famous for their poisonousness. They are all voracious predators. The more striking, like the *Pterois*, that with their colours remind potential predators of their venomous nature, hunt at night, feeding above all on crustaceans and small fish. Others, on the other hand, like the large *Scorpaenopsis diabolus* and *S. barbatus* and the terrible Stonefish, use incredible camouflage to ambush their prey. So well do they blend into their environment that they are often unrecognizable even on careful and close up scrutiny of the reef. They prevalently live in shallow waters and are thus a great danger for bathers who may step on them and be stung by the venomous spines. Excruciating pain is followed by swelling, breathing difficulties and in some cases even death.

136 - Tassled Scorpionfish (*Scorpaenopsis oxycephala*)

137

137 - Tassled Scorpionfish
    (*Scorpaenopsis oxycephala*)
138 - Stonefish (*Synanceia verrucosa*)
139 - Scorpionfish (*Scorpaenopsis sp.*)
140 - Lionfish (*Pterois volitans*)

138

141

141/143 - Lionfish (*Pterois volitans*)
144 - Clearfin Lionfish
    (*Pterois radiata*)

142

143

144

71

Antennaridae - Frogfish

Reef - nocturnal - solitary - carnivorous -
snorkelling/scuba - 0/30 m

Masters in the art of camouflage, the Frogfish become virtually invisible on whatever type of sea bed they find themselves. Their appearance is very strange: a spherical body covered with appendages, pectoral fins which can be used to "walk" on the seabottom, and the first ray of the dorsal fin metamorphosed into a "fishing rod" with a lure on the end of it. These animals spend most of their time lying motionless on the seabottom, moving the filiform appendage and waiting for a fish to be attracted by it and come near. The great elasticity of the Frogfish's mouth allows it to swallow prey longer than itself. Despite their disturbing appearance, these fish are completely harmless for man.

145, 146 - Frogfish (*Antennarius sp.*)

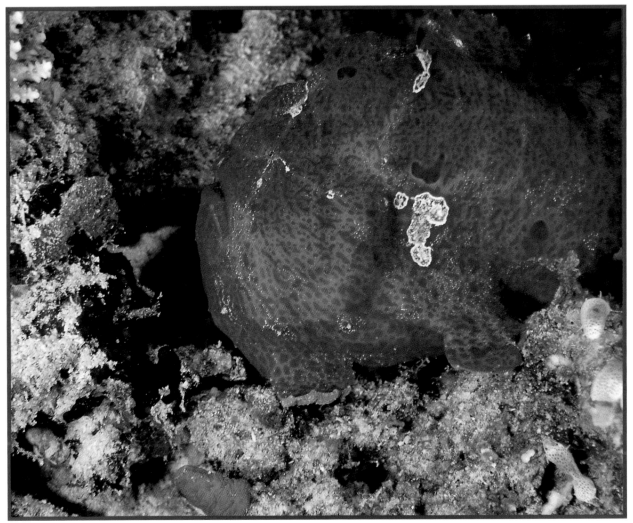

146

147

148

Platycephalidae - Flatheads

Benthonic - nocturnal - solitary - carnivorous - snorkelling/scuba - 5/40 m

Flatheads are encountered fairly frequently in the northern Red Sea, especially at the tip of Sinai, where they lie concealed on the bottom, partially covered with sand, ready to ambush fish who pass nearby. Their whole body is quite compressed and the head in particular is flat, with the lower jaw prominent, emphasising the aggressive air of this fish. In reality this fish is completely harmless for man, apart from a few pre-opercular spines which can cause painful stings if the fish is taken hold of. Flatheads live alone or in couples, sometimes lazily lying on top of one another. They seem to be particularly attracted to old sunken hulls and it is not rare to encounter them inside.

147/149 - Flathead (*Cociella crocodila*)

149

Synodontidae - Lizardfish

Benthonic - diurnal - solitary - carnivorous -
snorkelling/scuba - 3/20 m

The name comes from the particular form of the
head which resembles that of a reptile, with a large
mouth provided with sharp teeth. Lizardfish live
mainly on the sandy or muddy seabottom, burying
themselves to the point that only their eyes are visible. When a shrimp or a little fish passes by, they
suddenly dart out of their hiding place, capturing
their prey. Their perfect immobility makes them an
easy subject for underwater photography.

150

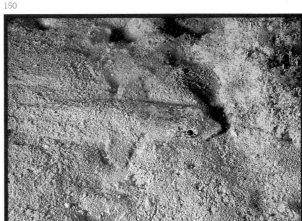

151

150/152 - Common Lizardfish (*Synodus variegatus*)

152

153

Holocentridae - Squirrelfish

Reef - nocturnal - carnivorous - scuba - 10/50 m

These are distinctive fish of a bright red colour with large eyes which testify to their nocturnal habits. During the day they take refuge in large holes and caverns protected from the light, whilst at night they come out in search of food, which is mostly made up of crustaceans. The largest representative of the family is the Sabre Squirrelfish (*Adioryx spinifer*), which can grow to 45 cm and has a pre-operculum bony spine. It lives alone or in small groups of 5-10 fish in the craggy depths of the reef, and swims to the scuba diver, who greatly arouses its curiosity, of its own accord.

153/155 - Sabre Squirrelfish (*Adioryx spinifer*)
156 - Blotcheye Soldierfish (*Myripristis murdjan*)

154

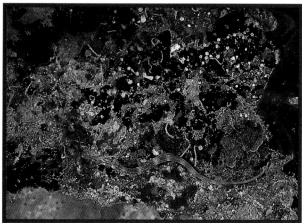

157

Syngnathidae - Pipefish

Reef - diurnal - solitary - carnivorous - snorkelling/scuba - 0/30 m

The name comes from the extremely slender and tapered form of the body, ending at the front in a long tubular snout. The body is armoured by a series of bony rings and its total length is not usually over 15-20 cm. The pipefish feeds on minute crustaceans which are swallowed by sucking in water through its trunk-like snout. The eggs laid by the female are incubated by the male in a special ventral pouch.

158

157 - Blackbreasted Pipefish *(Corythoichthys nigripectus)*
158, 159 - Gilded Pipefish *(Corythoichthys schultzi)*

Priacanthidae - Bigeyes

Reef - nocturnal - carnivorous - scuba - 10/50 m

These are very similar to the *Holocentridae* in appearance, colouring and nocturnal habits. They feed mostly on plankton like the larva of crustaceans and fish. Their colouring, normally of a bright and vivid red, can change in a few seconds to a more faded shade, or even become silvery grey. Recently examples of *Priacanthus hamrur* have been found off the Tunisian coasts, indicating probable migration through the Suez Canal.

160

161

160/162 - Goggle-Eye (*Priacanthus hamrur*)

162

163

164

Cirrhitidae - Hawkfish

Reef - diurnal - solitary - carnivorous -
snorkelling/scuba - 2/40 m

This is a small family of fish which pass their time resting on the reef or between the branches of the corals or the gorgonians. They are completely motionless and are thus an easy photographic subject. They are all carnivorous and feed on crustaceans and small fish. This group also shows the sex change phenomenon: first female and then, if necessary, male. The males are very territorial and have a little private harem of females.

166

167

163 - Longnose Hawkfish (*Oxycirrhites typus*)
164, 166/168 - Blackside Hawkfish (*Paracirrhites forsteri*)
165- Pixy Hawkfish (*Cirrhitichtys oxycephalus*)

165

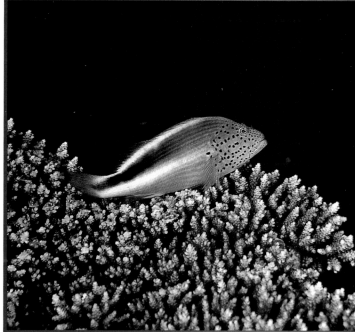

168

169

170

Apogonidae - Cardinalfish

Reef - nocturnal - solitary/gregarious - carnivorous - snorkelling/scuba - 5/50 m.

The common name of these fish derives from the red colouring which is a feature of many species, even if black, brown and yellow are also well represented. Most of the species remain hidden in holes or under cover all day, coming out at night to hunt the zooplankton or small crustaceans which live near the seabottom. Many Cardinalfish are solitary, others swim in couples or in small groups, but there are some small and semi-transparent species which form spectacular and enormous shoals at the top of the corals.
The male's role in reproduction is unusual: after having fertilized several hundred eggs just laid by the female, he takes them into his mouth where they remain for several days until they hatch.

169 - Largetooth Cardinalfish (*Cheilodipterus macrodon*)
170 - Cardinalfish (*Apogon sp.*)
171 - Golden Cardinalfish (*Apogon aureus*)

171

Ostraciidae - Trunkfish

Reef - diurnal - solitary - omnivorous -
snorkelling/scuba - 5/25 m.

Trunkfish owe their name and their funny appearance to the strong armour, composed of bony plates which makes up their body. They are thus slow swimmers and generally use only the anal and dorsal fins to move around, resorting to the caudal fin only in case of rapid flight. They feed on a large number of animal and vegetal organisms which live attached to the corals. Some species can give off a poisonous toxin when the fish is under stress. The poison can be lethal for other fish, but can also be lethal for the Trunkfish itself if it is in a limited amount of water.

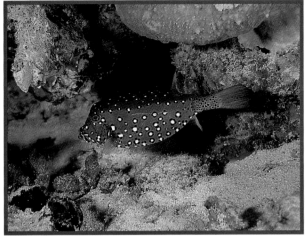

172

172 - Cube Trunkfish, juvenile (*Ostracion cubicus*)
173, 174 - Cube Trunkfish, adult (*Ostracion cubicus*)

173

174

Tetraodontidae - Pufferfish

Reef - diurnal - solitary - omnivorous - snorkelling/scuba - 5/25 m

Pufferfish get their name from their ability to puff themselves up when attacked or threatened. In these situations they pump water into a very stretchable diverticulum, located in the ventral area of the stomach, which increases the size of their body remarkably. Puffer produce a very powerful toxin which they accumulate in their tissues. Despite this their flesh is a much prized delicacy in the Orient, the famous Fugu, that only a very few experts know how to cook.

175, 176 - Masked Puffer (*Arothron diadematus*)

175

176

Diodontidae - Porcupinefish

Reef - nocturnal - solitary - carnivorous -
snorkelling/scuba - 5/25 m

Like the Pufferfishes, the members of this family
can swell up, and, in addition, they possess a further weapon of defense: the sharp spines which
cover their bodies. Normally these spines are flattened, but in the case of an attack, they are erected
and stand perpendicular to the body, and thus are
an excellent deterrent for attackers. Teeth which
are fused together in robust dental plates allow
these fish to grind the shells of shellfish and the
carapaces of crustaceans, and even to feed on
sea-urchins. Most of the species are nocturnal and
pass the day hidden in caves and crevices.

177 - Yellowspotted Burrfish (*Chilomycterus spilostylus*)
178 - Porcupinefish (*Diodon hystrix*)

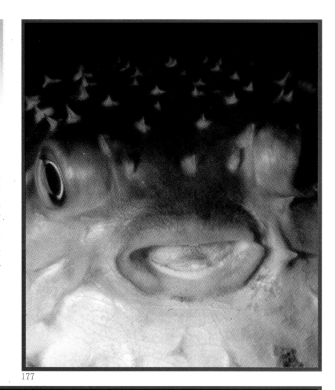

177

178

PORIFERA - SPONGES

When one speaks of sponges, the common bath sponge immediately springs to mind, whilst actually form, colour and consistency are very variable and many sponges may be totally unrecognizable for the novice. It is not easy to classify them underwater given that identification is very often made using a microscope to examine the calcium carbonate or silicaceous spicules which make up the skeleton. The sponges illustrated here are frequently met with in the Red Sea and are all *Demospongiae* or sponges with siliceous spicules embedded in a spongy structure called "spongin". Contrary to what was believed up to the eighteenth century, sponges are animals, not plants, even if they are very primitive, not having a clear differentiation between tissues and organs.

179

179 - *Leucetta chagosensis*
180 - Magnificant Fire Sponge (*Latrunculia corticata*)
181 - Siphon-Sponge (*Siphonochalina siphonella*)
182 - *Grayella cyathophora*

180

181

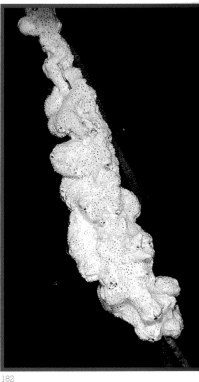
182

CNIDARIA

To this group belong all the extremely numerous animals which are polyps, that is small animals shaped like a calyx or goblet attached to a base, with series of stinging tentacles in a ring, and a mouth which opens in the middle of these. Polyps can be single, as in sea-anemones, or form large colonies. They can also be jellyfish-form, floating freely in the water, and often the two forms alternate with a fixed polyp producing a jellyfish asexually, the which, in its turn, sexually produces a polyp.

183, 184, 188 - Net Fire-coral
(*Millepora dichotoma*)

183

184

Hydrozoa

The hydrozoa are very well represented in the Red Sea, especially the well-known hard forms like "fire coral", so much so as to be the most widespread and characteristic species of the coral reefs in some areas.

The two main species are *Millepora dichotoma*, which is branching and of a browny-yellow colour with white tips, and *Millepora platyphylla*, which forms undulating vertical structures with a whitish upper edge. Both these species are confused with the corals although they are hydrozoa and armed with powerful stinging cells which cause painful "burns" if they come into contact with the skin. Another species which is to be found in crevices and fissures where wave motion is violent, is the beautiful *Distichopora violacea* which forms small colonies and is of a very intense violet-blue, also with white tips.

Plumed hydroids are completely different in appearance, they look like small flexible feather-shaped plants and are also very stinging. The best known species in the Red Sea is *Lytocarpus philippinus*.

185

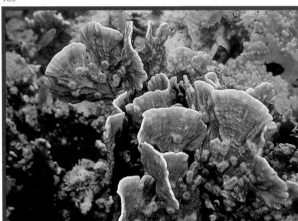

186

185 - Net Fire-coral, detail of stinging cells
      (*Millepora dichotoma*)
186 - Slab Fire-coral (*Millepora platyphylla*)
187 - Stylasterid Coral (*Distichopora violacea*)
189 - White stinging Sea-fan (*Lytocarpus philippinus*)

187

188

189

Scyphozoa (Jellyfish)

Jellyfish are among the least loved creatures of the sea due to the strong stinging power of some species. Really they are beautiful and fragile beings with a sophisticated system for catching their food. Jellyfish drift with the current or move slowly rhythmically contracting their umbrella, trailing long fine filaments armed with stinging cells (nematocysts) which at the least contact inject a powerful paralysing poison. Using this system they catch little planktonic organisms and tiny fish which swim near the surface. One of the most common in the Red Sea is *Aurelia aurita*, harmless for man, which has a quite flattened discoid structure and sometimes groups together in large shoals.

Cassiopea andromeda, the Upsidedown Jellyfish is very unusual. It lives with its umbrella against the seabottom and its tentacles upwards. They are easy to spot on the sandy sea bed in the shallows where they are a tasty titbit for turtles.

190, 192 - Moon Jellyfish (*Aurelia aurita*)
191 - Upsidedown Jellyfish (*Cassiopea andromeda*)

190

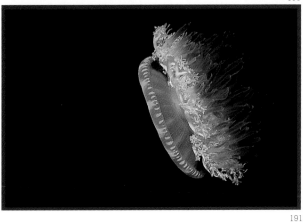

191

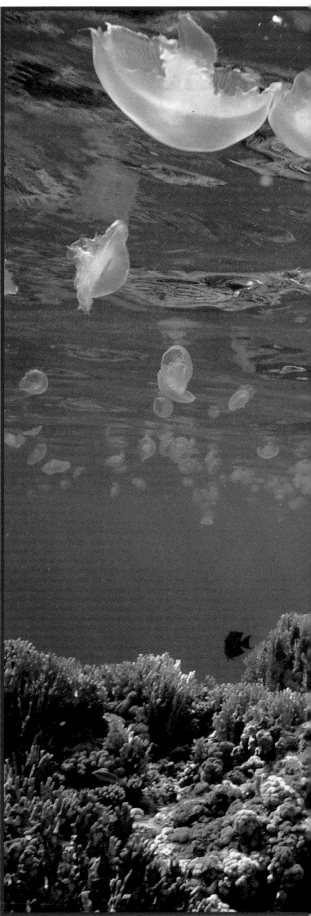

192

Anthozoa - *Octocorallia*

All the members of this group have eight tentacles and are always colonial.

GORGONIANS

These are colonies which form large fans positioned perpendicular to the current, so that the little polyps can catch the largest possible quantity of plankton. Thanks to their branching appearance and bright colours, they are one of the greatest attractions for divers. Their skeleton, apart from a few exceptions, is entirely horny, characterised by a certain flexibility. They live attached to the reef, usually along the precipitous sides and in caves where the water passes through and the current is channelled.

The large Giant Gorgonian Sea-fan *Subergorgia hicksoni* is that which reaches the largest dimensions, being able to grow to over 2 metres span. It grows where the current is quite strong, and provides support for crinoidea and some bivalvia.

Aqabaria splendens is, on the other hand, a yellow, very branchy and not very large gorgonian which only lives in calm waters.

Juncella juncea is very unusual in its whip-like form. It is a filiform gorgonian which grows at great depths, generally attached to hard substrates. The terminal part of the whip is slightly bent.

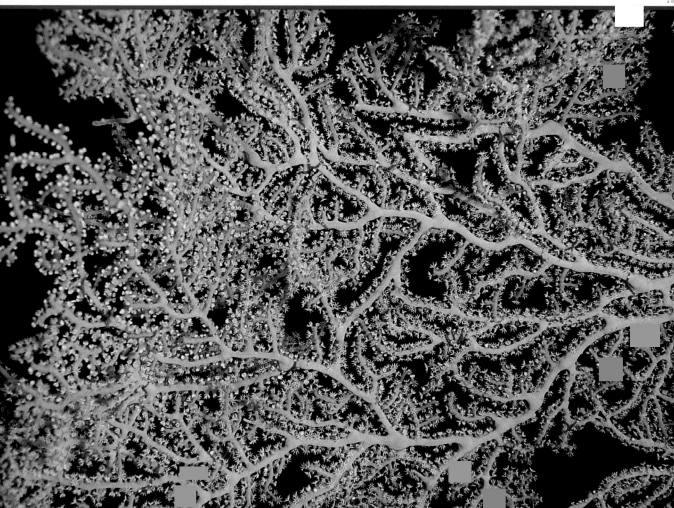

195

196

193 - Giant Gorgonian Sea-fan *(Subergorgia hicksoni)*
194, 196, 198 - *Aqabaria sp.*
195 - Gorgonian Sea-fan
197 - Whip Coral *(Juncella juncea)*

197

198

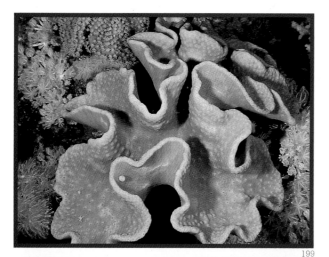

199

200

ALCYONACEA OR SOFT CORALS

The waters of the Red Sea are particularly spectacular due largely to the abundance of soft corals, which in quantity vie with the corals in certain areas, covering large stretches of reef.

The various families have such a different appearance that it is difficult to believe that they are closely related: one passes from slender bunches of coloured "flowers" to animals of a rubbery appearance and a uniformly grey colour. The polyps have eight tentacles (*octocorallia*), they feed on plankton carried by the current and can be retracted if necessary into the fleshy mass which makes up the structure of the colony, inside which there are small calcareous spicules.

The most loved, admired and photographed are the various species of *Dendronephtya*, usually known as alcyonacea. These have a branching structure of translucent matter in which the calcareous spicules can be seen quite well. The colours range from pink to dark red, from yellow to blue, from orange to violet.

The very common species *Lithophyton arboreum* is similar in appearance, though not translucent and of a uniform yellowish-white; it is often chosen as a refuge by small *Pomacentridae*.

Sarcophyton trocheliophorum is, on the other hand, similar to a greenish-grey sponge; it looks white when the polyps are evaginated with their corollas of tentacles extended.

201

202 203
204 205
206 207

199/202 - Sarcophyton Soft Coral
      (*Sarcophyton trocheliophorum*)
203, 204 - Sarcophyton Soft Coral (*Sarcophyton sp.*)
205 - Soft Coral (*Lithophyton arboreum*)
206, 207 - Xeniid Soft Coral (*Xeniidae*)
208 - Orange-pipe Coral (*Tubipora musica*)

208

209

209/213 - Soft Coral
(*Dendronephthya sp.*)

210

211

212

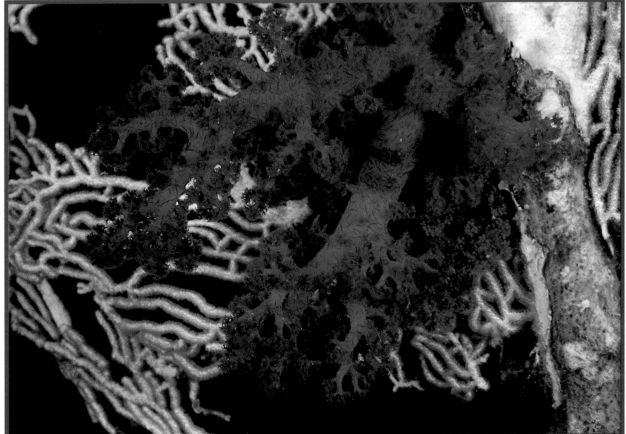

213

214

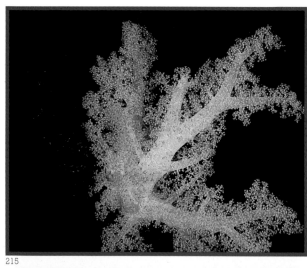

215

216

217

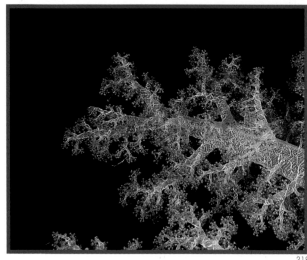

218

214/220 - Soft Coral (*Dendronephthya sp.*)

219

220

Hexacorallia

The most important characteristic of this group is the number of tentacles, being six or a multiple of six (*hexacorallia*). There are both solitary and colonial forms.

STONY CORALS

The madrepores or stony corals are the main builders of the coral reefs and are mostly colonial; their polyps have six tentacles or a multiple of six (*hexacorallia*). Every polyp is able to secrete calcium carbonate, which enlarges and strengthens the structure of the colony. The polyps feed on zooplankton and zooxanthella, algae which live in symbiosis with the corals and are largely responsible for their beautiful colours, which are often believed erroneously to be characteristic of the latter.

Their shape and size are incredibly varied: they can build very branched tree-like structures, towers and monoliths, large spherical masses, intricate serpentine labyrynths, broad umbrella canopies and many other forms. Corals offer a refuge to most of the coralline fauna, which seek protection from predators in between their branches and rigid structures.

Among the most intricate, and as a consequence, those which offer greater protection to fish are the acropores which often have violet and pinkish shades which they derive from zooxanthella. They are among the most widespread and numerous madrepores in all tropical seas.

Grandiose structures which are heavy and hard like real rocks belong, on the other hand, to the *Porites* genus; they often house polychaetes and bivalves inside them.

The surface of the *Pachyseris* genus is scoured with an infinite series of little furrows, as if the madrepore had been "combed".

The *Favites* genus takes its name from its honeycomb structure.

Differing from the other corals which are generally colonial, those belonging to the *Fungia* genus (mushroom corals) are made up of one polyp, except some species which are, however, only made up of a few polyps. There name derives from the likeness of their numerous septa to the lamellas of fungae. *Fungia repanda* has a discoid form and is often mistaken for a dead madrepore by novices, as during the day it shows no movement whatsoever and its tentacles are not visible. At night, however, the tentacles come out from the interstices between the lamellas and the polyp feeds on plankton. The corals of the *Dendrophyllia* genus are like beautiful flowers with yellow or pink corollae; during the day they draw their crown of tentacles into the polyp. They are common on the ceilings of dark grottos at a certain depth. Also in the depths it's possible to observe the beautiful branching colonies of *Tubastrea*, which are very fragile and break easily if bumped; their tentacles are evaginated at night, making them look like flowering plants.

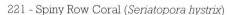

221 - Spiny Row Coral (*Seriatopora hystrix*)
222 - *Pocillopora sp.*
223/225 - Staghorn Coral (*Acropora sp.*)
226 - *Gardineroseris sp.*
227, 228 - *Pachyseris sp.*
229 - *Galaxea fascicularis*
230, 231 - *Fungia sp.*
232 - *Fungia sp.* showing the tentacles which come out from between the calcareous lamellas during the hours of darkness.
233 - *Porites sp.*
234 - *Favites sp.*
235 - *Diploastrea heliopora*

221

222

223

224

225

226

227

228

229

230

231

232

233

234

235

236

237

236, 237 - *Fungia sp.*
238 - *Dendrophyllia sp.*
239 - *Tubastrea sp.*

238

239

ACTINIARIA - SEA ANEMONES

Numerous species belong to this group and they are all solitary and do not have a skeleton. They are carnivores and make use of stinging cells on their tentacles to capture small organisms such as fish and crustaceans, which after having been paralysed by the poison, are quickly drawn into the mouth which opens in the middle of the tentacles and devoured.

The most common in the Red Sea is *Gyrostoma helianthus* which lives between the surface and 40 metres depth, growing to a remarkable size. It almost always is host to a couple of Clownfishes (*Amphiprion bicinctus*) which because of their protective mucus, are immune to its poison. The lower part of this sea anemone has a very bright colouring which varies from pink to scarlet.

240, 241 - Sea Anemones *(Actiniaria)* - Family: *Stoicactidae*

240

241

ANELLIDA (Worms) - Polychaeta

This group numbers thousands of species which are subdivided into two main categories: mobile types and types which live attached to the substrate. The first, of vermiform appearance have a series of tufts of bristles (*setae*) positioned on each segment. In the case of the Fire-Worm (*Hermodice carunculata*), these setae cause intense pain if they come into contact with the skin. The sedentary types have a totally different appearance, looking like little flowers or tufts of feathers. They live inside a thin tube which they themselves secrete and which is fixed to the substrate or in some cases completely buried in the calcium carbonate of the large brain corals. They feed by filtering water through their showy and often coloured branchial tufts, retaining the plankton. If disturbed they withdraw instantaneously into their tube.

242, 243 - Christmas Tree Worm
    (*Spirobranchus giganteus*)
244 - Fire-Worm (*Hermodice carunculata*)
245 - Fan-Worm (*Sabellastarte sanctijosephi*)

242

243

244

245

CRUSTACEA

The body of most crustaceans is covered with a strong protective shell which, being rigid, does not grow as the animal develops. Thus periodically they must substitute the old carapace with a new one, a particularly delicate period as the new protection is not initially sufficiently hard, and until it is they are at the mercy of predators. Most crustaceans have separate sexes and fertilisation is mostly internal. In the life cycle of some hermaphrodite species sex change takes place.

Several species of lobster live in the Red Sea and they are easy to sight at night in the shallow waters of the reef. The Painted Crayfish (*Panulirus versicolor*) is one of the largest and can be recognised by its bright colouring: green and white stripes with pink and blue details.

Hermit crabs have soft and undefended abdomens and have to find an abandoned shell in which to establish their home. The Spotted Hermit Crab (*Dardanus tinctor*) often carries a few sea anemones on the shell, as their stinging tentacles are a deterrent for predators.

CLEANER SHRIMP

Cleaner Shrimps (Stenopus hispidus) *are among the most photographed by divers because of their beautiful red and white stripes. These little animals feed on parasites which trouble fish and crustaceans. In order to obtain their food in this way, Cleaner Shrimps organise real "cleaning stations", as some fish also do, where they pass much time waving their long white antennae and waiting for clients. When one approaches, the Shrimp first starts to lightly brush it with its antennae in order to restrain its aggressiveness and reassure it, and then it sets to work to eliminate the parasites present on the skin, in the gills and in the mouth.*

Normally these Shrimps live in couples which remain together all their lives.

246 - Painted Crayfish (*Panulirus versicolor*)
247 - Spotted Hermit Crab (*Dardanus tinctor*)
248 - Cleaner Shrimp (*Stenopus hispidus*)

246

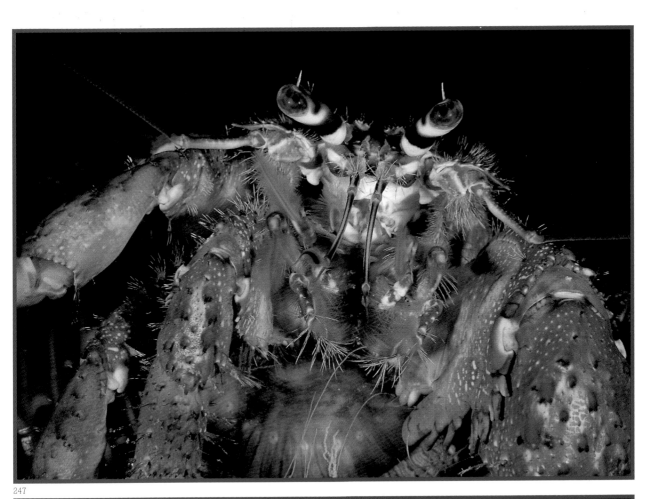

247

248

MOLLUSCS

It is difficult to remain indifferent to the beauty of shells. In few other creatures has nature indulged herself in such a large variety of shapes and colours, to which is often added a lustre which makes them into real jewels, greatly coveted by collectors. However, it must not be forgotten that these are living animals and thus everywhere in the Red Sea the collecting of them is banned.

Prominent among the various groups are that of the Gastropods, which are provided with a single shell, often spiral, or have no shell (nudibranchs) and that of the *Bivalvia*, with the shell made up of two parts or "valves".

Gastropods
Prosobranchia (Shells)

The *Prosobranchia* are partly carnivores, hunting live prey or feeding on dead animals, and partly herbivores. In order to feed, both use their radula, a kind of tongue made up of a toothed chitinous plate, with which the first can pierce the shells of other molluscs, whilst the herbivores use it to scrape off the algae they feed on. Cowries must be enumerated among the most beautiful gastropods with their marvellous shiny ovoidal shells. The most common cowrie is the Panther Cowrie (*Cypraea pantherina*), which like other molluscs has nocturnal habits.

The cone-shells are also very beautiful, but they should be looked at and not touched as some species, as Textile Cone (*Conus textile*) are able to let fly a very poisonous dart which in some cases has even caused the death of the collector.

249 - Tapestry Turban (*Turbo petholatus*)
250 - *Trochus dentatus*
251, 252 - Panther Cowrie (*Cypraea pantherina*)
253 - Auger Shell (*Terebra maculata*)
254 - Textile Cone (*Conus textile*)

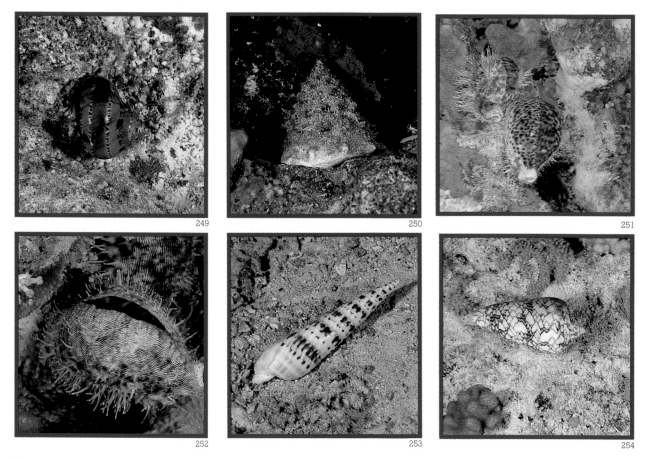

249

250

251

252

253

254

Gastropods - *Opisthobranchia*

NUDIBRANCHIA (NUDIBRANCHS)

These molluscs without a shell look like little slugs and have bright and beautiful colours which make them a favourite subject for photographers. The object of their showy and bright livery is to inform enemies that they are unappetizing. To this end they have developed various strategies. Some possess special glands which secrete repellent substances, others manage to retain in their tissues the stinging cells of the hydrozoa on which they feed, becoming stinging themselves. Others still, cover their external tissue with the calcareous or siliceous spicules of the sponges on which they feed, constructing a real shell.

Diving on sandy seabottoms during the night, one can see the beautiful Spanish Dancer (*Hexabranchus sanguineus*), a large, bright red nudibranch, about 15 cm long, which can swim about by twisting itself around, in movements which resemble elegant dance steps.

255, 256 - Spanish Dancer (*Hexabranchus sanguineus*)
257 - *Phyllidia sp.*
258, 259 - *Chromodoris quadricolor*
260 - *Halgerda willeyi*

255

256

257

258

259

260

TRIDACNIDAE - GIANT CLAMS

Anyone swimming in shallow water will be struck by a strange shell with undulating edges, positioned upwards, so that from the opening between the valves, the mantle of the animal sticks out ; these are tridacnidae or giant clams. They may take on the most varied and marvellous colours, from brown to green, turquoise to yellow. This colouring derives from microscopic algae (zooxanthella) which are "cultivated" by the mollusc, which then feeds on a part of them. The tridacnidae are also called Killer Clams because the largest species in the Indo-Pacific, the individual clams of which can reach 250 kilograms in weight, is accused of having held down pearl-fishers who had put a foot between the open valves by mistake, causing them to drown.

Bivalvia

The two valves are joined by an elastic ligament which functions as a hinge. Adductor muscles close the shell and are powerful enough to resist the force of two strong hands, though octopuses and starfish often manage to force them open.
Bivalves all live near the seabottom, buried in the sand, attached to hard substrates or fixed to gorgonians. Most species feed by filtering water by means of a two-siphon system: the "inhalent" one draws in the water, the other, which is "exhalent" expels it after the gills have retained the plankton.

261, 264, 266 - Giant Clam *(Tridacna maxima)*
262 - Scallop *(Pedum spondylium)*
263 - True Oyster *(Lopha cristagalli)*
265 - Thorny Oyster *(Spondylus sp.)*

261

262

263

264

265

266

267

ECHINODERMS

This group unites animals which appear to be very different with a few common characteristics, for example the five-rayed symmetry which is very evident in the *Asteroidea* (starfish), *Ophiuroidea* (brittle stars) and in the *Crinoidea* (Feather Stars), and the presence of an internal skeleton made up of calcareous plates. The sexes in the echinoderms are usually separate, even if some species are hermaphrodite.

Crinoidea (Feather Stars)

Pretty to look at and often brightly coloured, the *Crinoidea* are made up of a small central body from which branch off feathered arms, which though they are very fragile, are easily regenerated. On the bottom half of the body there are short cirri (special clinging feet) with which they walk and cling to the substrate. They are typically nocturnal animals which pass the daylight hours rolled up in a ball and hidden in the crevices of the reef. At night they leave their refuge and climb up to the high parts of the reef, or onto gorgonians, where the current is strong, bringing the plankton on which they feed.

267/271, 274 - Feather Stars (*Crinoidea*)

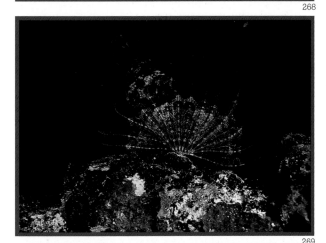

268

269

270   271

Ophiuroidea (Brittle Stars)

The ophiurids or brittle stars bear a close resemblance to the starfish, but differ from them in their small discoid body and their slender serpentine arms, which in some families are smooth and in others they have numerous sharp spines which easily penetrate the flesh if touched. The ophiurids usually live hidden in crevices, under the madrepores or clinging to gorgonians or sponges and most of them have nocturnal habits.

Astroboa nuda, the Basket Star, stands out clearly from the others because of its large size and unusual form. It can be seen almost exclusively at night, when it leaves its daytime hiding place and climbs up to the exposed parts of the reef, in order to position itself in the current. Here it opens out its long arms, which are very branched and provided with little cirri, with which it catches its food. It can reach a metre in diameter and if it is illuminated, it immediately folds in its arms and rolls up, reducing itself to a very intricate "basket" of 20 or so centimetres.

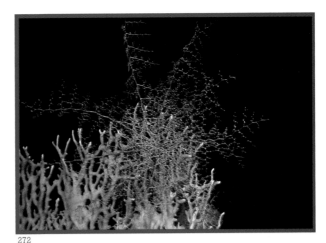

272

273

272 - Basket Star (*Astroboa nuda*)
273 - Purple Brittle Star (*Ophiothrix purpurea*)

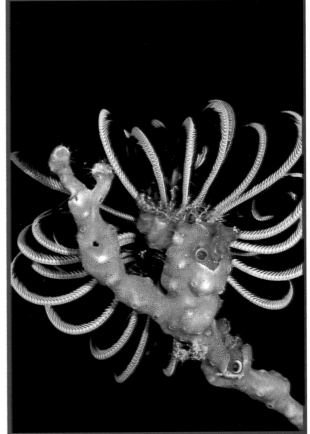

274

CROWN OF THORNS STARFISH

The Crown of Thorns starfish (Acanthaster plan-ci) gets its name from the great number of spines which cover its surface and it can give a very painful sting which may cause bad infection. This starfish devours the polyps of the madrepores, killing the corals. It has very few enemies, being preyed upon above all by a large mollusc, Charonia tritonis, which is not very common. A few years ago there was a population explosion of these starfish on the Great Barrier Reef of Australia, which has destroyed large tracts of reef. It was no good chopping the starfish up underwater, because from every piece a new starfish was generated, exactly like the devilish personages in certain science fiction stories.

Asteroidea (Starfish)

Starfish are carnivores and some species are great predators of bivalves which they manage to open by gripping the shell with their arms and exerting an extremely strong pull on the two valves until they open. At this point the starfish evaginate their stomach through their mouth, and insert it between the two halves of the shell, digesting the unfortunate bivalve on the spot.

Many starfish have an incredible regenerative capacity which enables them to re-form arms or any part of the body which is missing. *Linckia multifora*, the Comet Starfish, is a master of this art, which it also uses to reproduce asexually, dividing its body into two pieces, each of which regenerates the missing part. The "comet" starfish which one sometimes sees are nothing but starfish with a broken-off arm which is regenerating a new star.

275 - Pin Cushion Starfish (*Choriaster granulosus*)
276 - *Fromia monilis*
277 - *Fromia sp.*
278 - Comet Starfish (*Linckia multifora*)

279 - Egyptian Starfish *(Gomophia egyptiaca)*
280/282 - Crown of Thorns *(Acanthaster planci)*

275

276

277

278

114

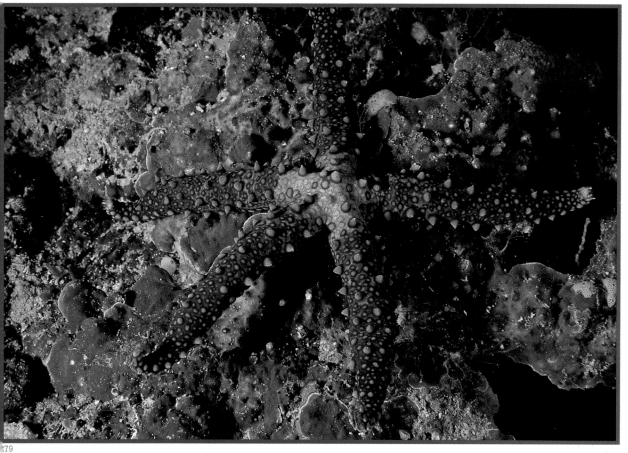

279

280

282

281

Echinoidea (Sea Urchins)

These echinoderms usually have a globular form, even if some species are discoid, like the sea urchins which live under the sand. Their body, closed in a compact shell, is covered with mobile spines, whilst the mouth, surrounded by five strong teeth opens underneath to allow the animal to crop algae and the detritus on which it feeds.

The most widespread is the Diadem Urchin (*Diadema setosum*) which has long and fragile spines and which appears above all at night. *Asthenosoma varium*, the Pin Cushion Urchin, a red sea urchin covered with little white knobs, is dangerous because its spines are armed with sacs full of poison. *Heterocentrotus mammillatus*, sometimes called the Slate-pencil Urchin, has, on the other hand, large and thick triangular spines and lives in shallow water where the robust nature of its spines allows it to withstand the turbulence of the waves. Its name comes from the fact that in the past the spines were used to write on blackboards.

283, 285, 286 - Diadem Urchin (*Diadema setosum*)
284 - Pin Cushion Urchin (*Asthenosoma varium*)
287 - Slate-pencil Urchin (*Heterocentrotus mammillatus*)
288 - *Tripneustes gratilla*
289 - Pin Cushion Urchin (*Asthenosoma varium*)
 detail of the ampullae full of poison

283

284

285

286

287

288

289

Holothuroidea
(Sea Cucumbers)

These are echinoderms of an elongate form, similar to a large cucumber, which live on sandy or gravelly sea beds. Here they find food using their tentacles which are arranged in a circle round the mouth. Some *holothuroidea* are filterers, but the greater number pass their time eating large quantities of coral sand, from which they extract the organic substances on which they feed. It has been calculated that the holothuroidea present in hectare of sea bed are capable of sifting 150 tons of sand in a year. An unusual defense strategy of many species consists of voluntarily expelling either entrails, which grow back in a few months, or a mass of fine white filaments which gel on contact with the water, becoming very sticky.

290, 291 - *Thelenota ananas*
292 - Striated Sea Cucumber *(Bohadschia graeffei)*
293 - Sticky Snake Sea Cucumber *(Opheodesma grisea)*
294 - Grampus *(Grampus griseus)*

290

292

291   293

CETACEA

Despite their appearance which is similar overall to that of fish, cetaceans are mammals. About 55 million years ago they started a long evolution process which has transformed them from small terrestrial quadrupeds to highly efficient aquatic animals of a remarkable intelligence. In the Red Sea the most common cetaceans are the Bottlenosed Dolphin various species of Stripped Dolphin and the *Grampus*.

The Bottlenosed Dolphin are quite large dolphins, about three metres long, characterised by a grey colour which is darker on their backs. They are very agile swimmers and can reach a remarkable speed, sometimes swimming at over 30 km/h. Like all cetaceans they come up to the surface to breath and are able to stay under in apnoea for up to eight minutes. The Bottlenosed Dolphin feeds mostly on fish, but its diet can be varied according to the availability of prey (squids, prawn, octopuses, crustaceans). Their complex and fascinating social organisation and their vocalisation which they use to communicate, are among the most studied aspects of this species.

This dolphin is widespread, existing throughout the world and is well known to the public at large, being the most common cetacean in dolphinariums.

295 - Striped Dolphin (*Stenella sp.*)
296 - Bottlenosed Dolphin (*Tursiops truncatus*)

295   296

TURTLES

One of the most thrilling underwater encounters is that with a turtle. In nature they have few enemies, limited to a few sharks, like the tiger shark, which is able to break their shell with its extremely strong jaws. Man, on the other hand, has always hunted turtles relentlessly for their meat, carapace and oil, which is used in cosmetics as ingredients for creams and in medicine to cure lung troubles. They have been hunted to such an extent that today they are considered an endangered species and in serious danger of extinction.

In the course of their evolutionary history they have adapted, along with few other reptiles, to the sea environment. This long and complex process, which has involved a series of important anatomical and physiological modifications, allows these animals to pass all their lives in the sea, except

297 - Typical tracks made by a turtle which has come up on the beach to lay its eggs.
298/300 - Imbricated Turtle (*Eretmochelis imbricata*)

297

298

during the reproduction period when the female must return to land to lay her eggs under the sand.

One of the most fascinating aspects of these unique reptiles is their extraordinary orientation capacity. When the females reach sexual maturity, they always return to lay their eggs on the very beach where they were born, and the little turtles, when just hatched, are capable of reaching the sea, attracted by its reflected light.

In the Red Sea there are several species of sea turtle, among which the more common are the Green Turtle and the Imbricated Turtle.

299

00

CORAL WORLD

Seven kilometers south of Eilat, one of the major attractions of the city is the Coral Beach Nature Reserve. The complex of Coral World was inaugurated in March of 1975 and has continued to grow in size and wealth throughout the years.

At present it includes a large circular structure inaugurated in May 1982 which encloses a replica of the reef, three large pools with sharks, giant tortoises and sea turtles, an Aquarium with a Marine Museum and the large Underwater Observatory which goes down below the surface of the sea for four and a half meters. The pool for sharks was added in 1982. It holds 800 cubic meters of water and is constantly refurnished with fresh sea water. The large sharks which slowly swim around inside can be observed through four large windows. The circular structure nearby is an enourmous aquarium which contains about 300,000 liters of water and in which the coral reef with all its characteristics has been faithfully reproduced. Twelwe large windows make it possible to admire the fish that live near the reef in all their varicolored splendor. As if in a silent film, the surrealistic colors and shapes of the tropical fish move to and from before our eyes. The wonders of this underwater world continue in the aquarium, where over a hundred species of fish are to be seen, as well as examples of sponges and corals and hundreds of species of invertebrates, all from the gulf of Eilat. Via a special "Natural Water Flow System", the water is pumped directly from the ocean into a reservoir from which it flows by gravity and fills each of the twenty-three tanks, twenty-four hours a day, thus naturally introducing the plancton which the various species need. And then, lastly, comes the Submarine Observatory, which can be reached via a boardwalk a hundred meters long built over the water. The proximity of the coral reef to the coast has made it possible to construct this observatory so close to the beach. Built in iron, it weighs about a hundred tons and is set four and a half meters below the level of the sea. From the crystal windows one can see the coral reef - the real thing and not a copy - in all its silent and majestic beauty. The water is always exceptionally clear, thanks to the fact that it almost never rains and thus prohibits the formation of sand sendiment while facilitating the growth of coral.

The Underwater Observatory

The crenellated walls of the Crusader fort on Coral Island

CORAL ISLAND

Emerging from the crystal waters of the gulf as if by magic, barely one and a half kilometers from Taba, this granitic island is surrounded by the reef and its silhouette is echoed by the crenellations of a Crusader castle.

The Arabs have always called it Jezirat el Faroun, or Island of the Pharaoh, for there was doubtless an Egyptian settlement here in the 15th century B.C. The Romans and the Byzantines fortified, it more than once and the Crusaders built the castle whose crennellated walls still stand.

The crusader knight Renaud de Châtillon, in emulation of Jehoshaphat whose expedition for Ophir probably left from here, had his ships transported to this spot on camels through the Arava Depression, intending then to set off on his conquest of what is now Arabia.

English name index

This index and that which follows refer to the number or letter next to the photographs

Latin name index

INDEX